BY: JIM DAVIS

BALLANTINE BOOKS • NEW YORK

20 19 18 17 16 15 14 13

Contents

Garfield was created to entertain. Given that and our feeling that there's a lot more to Garfield than a seven inch newspaper format will allow, the artists at Paws, Incorporated, and I put the furry fellow on the rack and stretched him to the limits of our imaginations.

It occurred to us there were elements of Garfield's complex personality that may well have been established in his previous lives…a cat's proverbial "nine lives." It was an exciting premise, one which consumed the staff and brought out the best in everyone. Many all-nighters and hundreds of hours of conceptual discussion went into this book.

This is a different book. It is dedicated to the Garfield philosophy of pure entertainment. I am also dedicating this book to the staff whose talents and courage made this bold statement possible: Neil Altekruse, Gary Barker, Kevin Campbell, Jim Clements, Doc Davis, Larry Fentz, Mike Fentz, Valette Hildebrand, Dave Kühn and Ron Tuthill.

IN THE BEGINNING...

Written by: Jim Davis
Illustrated by: Paws Staff

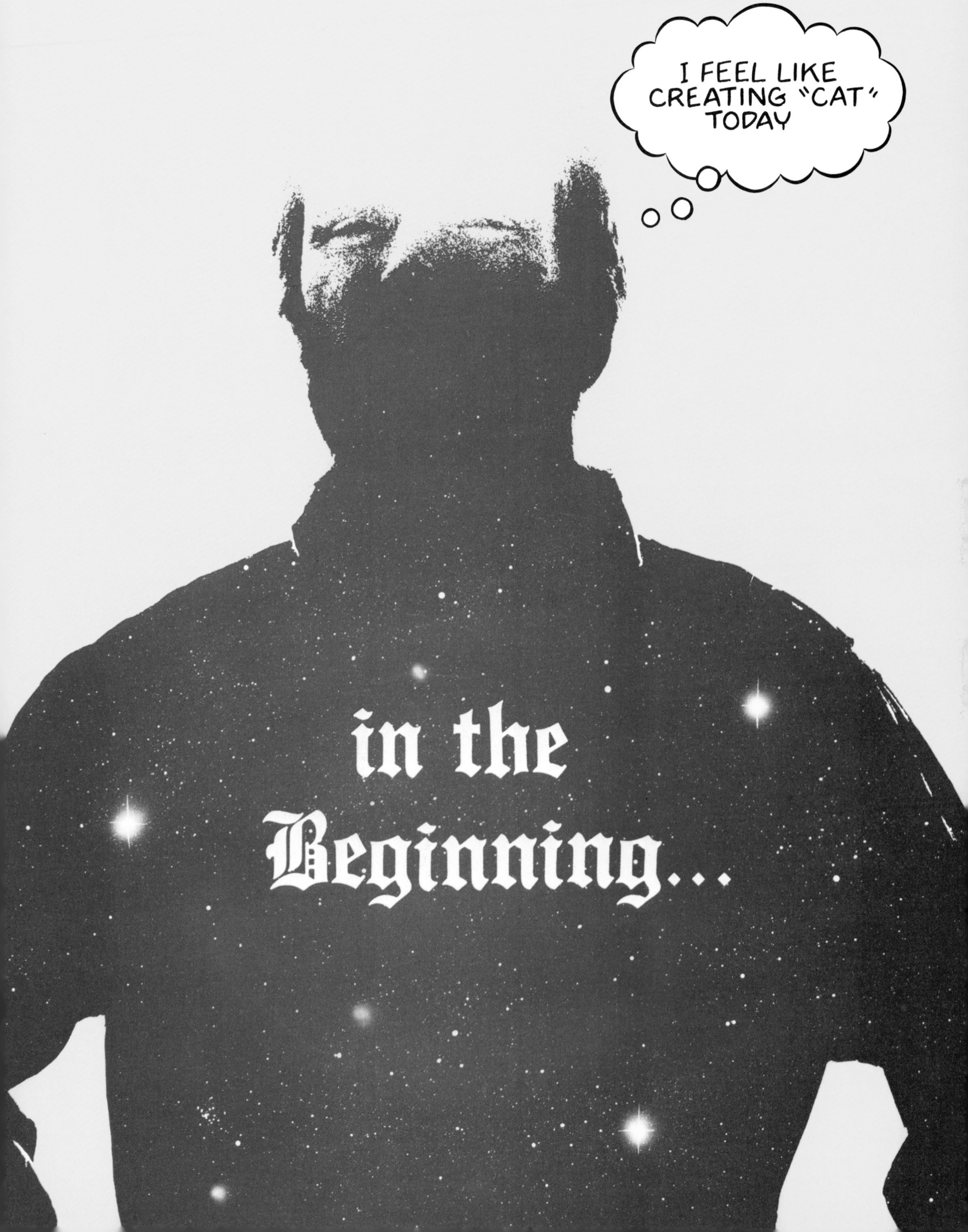
I FEEL LIKE CREATING "CAT" TODAY
in the Beginning...

CAVE CAT
Written by: Jim Davis
Illustrated by: Jim Davis, Mike Fentz, and Larry Fentz

WHONGO

CAT!

"CAT" WAS CAVEMAN FOR "DARN"

FOOM!

FOOM?

FOOM!

NO, NO, NO, HMMM, MEYOW?

MEYOW!

MEYOW, MEYOW, MEYOW

THINGS WERE PRETTY MUCH THE SAME THEN AS NOW...

EXCEPT FOR THE FIRE-BREATHING MICE

THINGS WERE ALSO PRETTY QUIET...

Z

FOOM!

GABUNG! GABUNG! GABUNG!

BIG BOB SLOBBERED

AND RAN AWAY

GABUNG! GABUNG!

CAVE CAT GAVE BIG BOB A PIECE OF HIS MIND

SNOOGA POP-POP OO CUR POOP

ALAS, BIG BOB RETURNED WITH THE WORLD'S FIRST (AND LAST) FRAP TREE

GABUNG! GABUNG!

HE WANTED TO PLAY FETCH

POO!

THUS, THE WORLD'S FIRST (AND LAST) CAVE CAT BOUGHT THE FARM FOR FAILING TO FIELD A FETCHED FRAP TREE...

ON WITH GARFIELD'S SECOND LIFE

THE VIKINGS
Written by: Jim Davis and Mike Fentz
Illustrated by: Mike Fentz

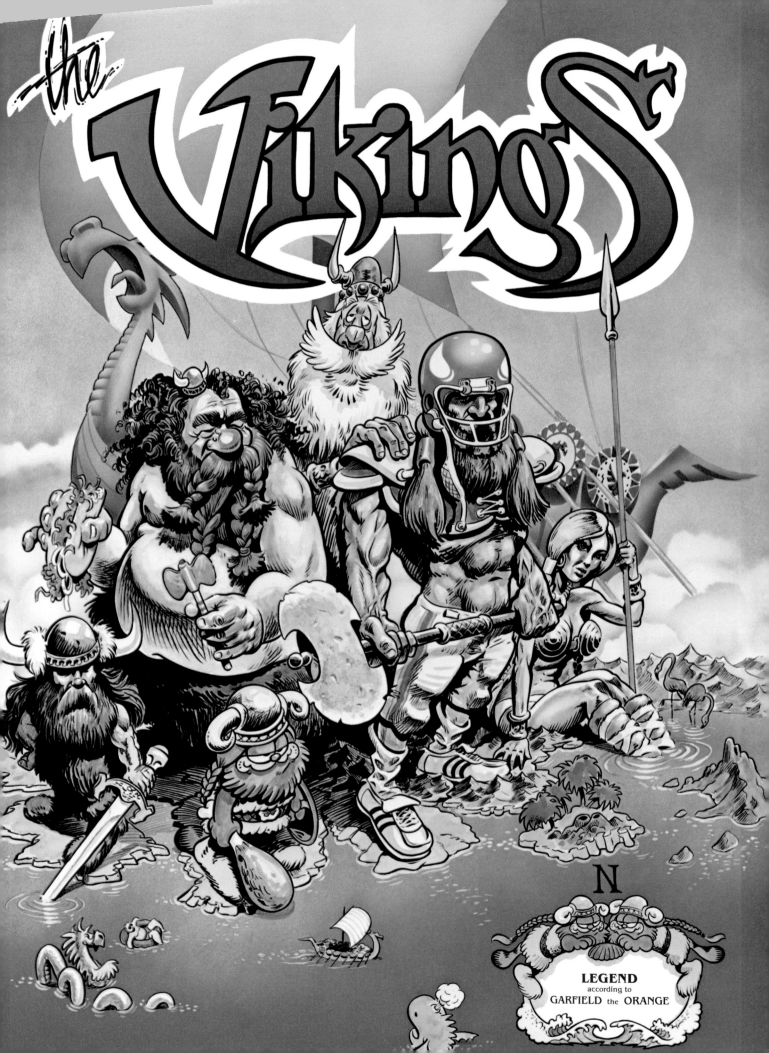

the VikingS

N

LEGEND
according to
GARFIELD the ORANGE

It was especially lovely and warm that day in the spring of 1984 . . . Lovely and warm for the polar ice cap, that is.

Balmy, spring breezes wafted over the permafrost, and walruses chirped their delight. They had no idea that their landscape was suddenly about to change.

CHIRP

CHIRP CHIRP

A huge iceberg broke off the polar ice shelf . . .

SPLASH!

. . . and floated through the Davis Strait, down the St. Lawrence Seaway . . .

. . . up Lake Superior, and down the St. Croix River to a point just outside St. Paul, Minnesota . . .

. . . where it came to rest against a grassy riverbank.

As the late summer sun beat down, the huge chunk of ice heaved a mighty sigh. Gradually...magically...human form sprouted from the core of the melting iceberg.

HELGA! LONG TIME, NO SEE

CAN IT, DWARF

GROAN, MY ICEBERG HAD A LUMP IN IT

I'M SO HUNGRY I COULD GRAZE

THAT'S THE LAST TIME I TRAVEL COACH

I'D KILL FOR A TWINKIE

Believe it or not, reviving from a state of suspended animation were real live Vikings, who had set off on a voyage across the North Sea in the year 984.

The iceberg also released the Petrified Weasel of Booga. The Holy trinket that symbolized the unity and power of this Viking clan. The weasel was once a pet of Booga the Bad, the Viking's patron saint.

The Vikings, being a tight-knit fraternity, greeted each other in the usual manner.

Not knowing they had just arisen from a nap of a thousand years, the Vikings set off to pillage another village. They soon came upon St. Paul.

Beaten, frustrated and battle-weary, the Vikings re-grouped to assess the situation and take stock of themselves.

MAYBE THEY'RE RIGHT. MAYBE WE SHOULD MAKE SOMETHING OF OURSELVES

The infamous Vikings had themselves shorn of their noble locks, their honor and their pride. They were so good, the barber gave them each a sucker.

SNIP! SNIP!

CLIP! CUT!

Determined to conform to this strange new civilization, they took adult education courses at night to learn useful trades.

 Garfield the Orange: a house cat.

 Lars: a life insurance salesman.

 Helga: an advertising executive.

 Björn: a junior high school teacher.

 Smitty: a plumber.

 Sven: a factory worker.

Once a proud fighting force, the Vikings donned the uniforms of the working force, rented an apartment and easily slipped into the everyday hum drum, rum tum, ho hum, make-an-honest-living scene.

As they grew accustomed to the routine of simply existing in 20th Century society, their primal ways faded away to no more than a shadowy memory from the past. Lifeless, listless and lackluster by now, they surrendered to the tedium of life in a rut.

HELLO... CHOMP, MUNCH... NO, DIS AIN'T DA LADY OF DA HOUSE... MUNCH, SLURP... DUH, HOW MUCH DOES DEY COST? BURP!

WHO FORGOT TO PUT THE TOILET SEAT DOWN AGAIN?

TAKE MY PAWN EN PASSANT, HUH? HOW'D YOU LIKE ME TO CASTLE YOUR NOSE AND YOUR RIGHT EAR?

IN SPORTS NEWS... THE VIKINGS WERE SLAUGHTERED BY THE BEARS LAST NIGHT

CRASH!

SIGH

SQUEEK! SQUEEK!

Alone and bored, Garfield knocked around the apartment.

BORED, BORED, BORED, ETC.

MAYBE RUMMAGING THROUGH OUR TRUNK OF TRINKETS WILL GET ME OUT OF THIS DEEP FUNK

MY HELMET!

AND LEGGIN'S!

...AND OUR PETRIFIED WEASEL!

Then something magical happened. The weasel started to glow, and with the impact of a thousand lightning bolts, Garfield the House Cat transformed back into Garfield the Orange.

SNAP! POP! SCHWAPP!

BOOGA!

Freed of the mindless mental agony of the assembly line, Sven did something we'd all like to do. He sought out the time clock and gave the mechanical monitor a taste of the cold steel of his broadsword.

Reunited, the Vikings instinctively ran far, far to the north woods, never to be seen again...

...It was especially lovely and warm that day in the spring of 2984...

I WAS GAINFULLY EMPLOYED IN MY THIRD LIFE. I LEARNED A LOT FROM THAT EXPERIENCE. I'VE SWORN OFF WORK

BABES AND BULLETS
Written by: Ron Tuthill
Illustrated by: Kevin Campbell

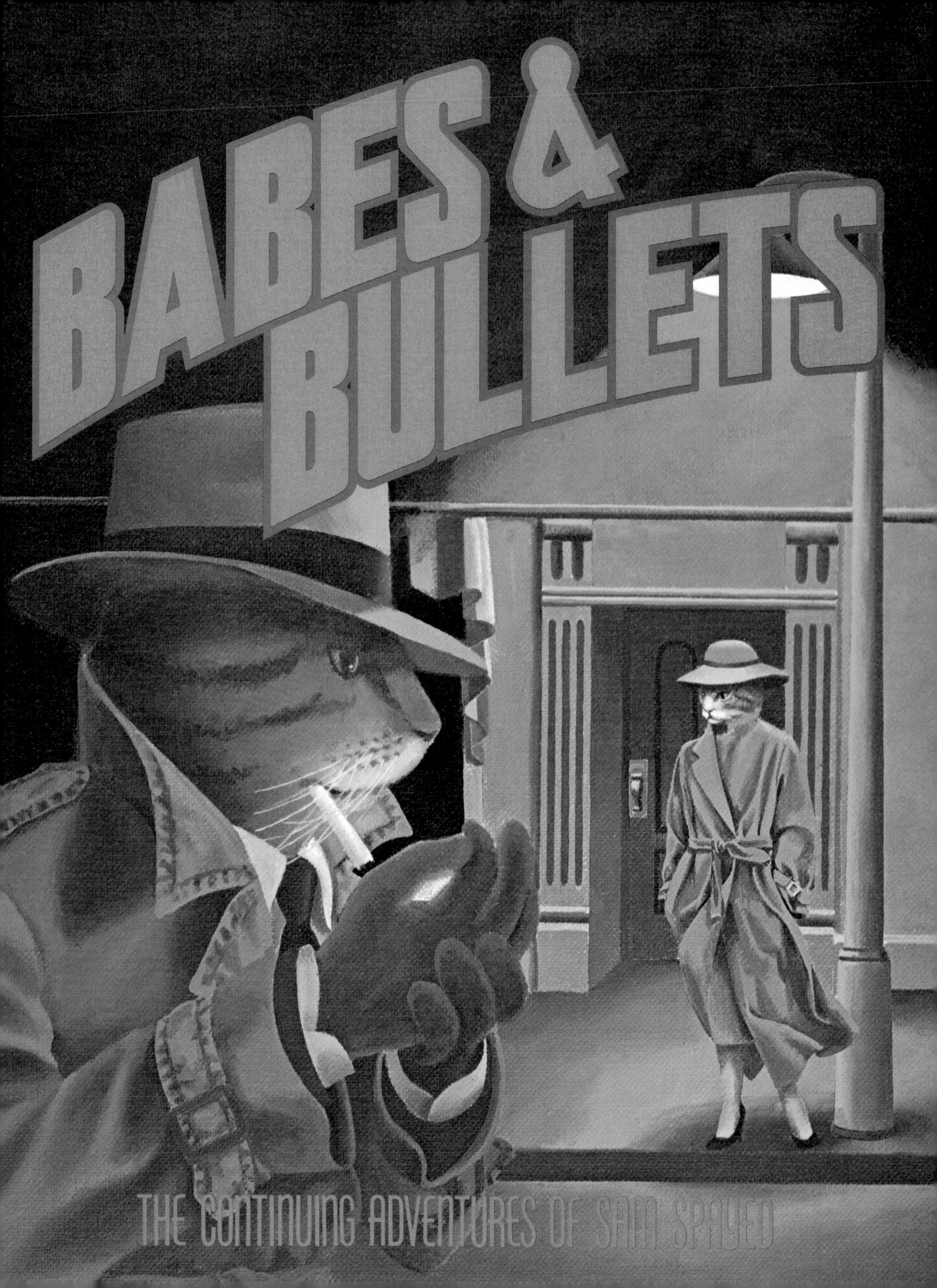
BABES &
BULLETS
THE CONTINUING ADVENTURES OF SAM SPAYED

The dust had to be an inch thick on my desk. A thick layer of papers was forming around the base of the trash can. An empty bottle of scotch lay on the floor next to the couch where I had a business engagement the night before.

"Coffee, Sam?"

Kitty wasn't much on keeping an office clean, but she *could* make a great cup of coffee. I still remember the day she came in looking for work. The dust had to be a half inch thick on my desk. A thin layer of papers was forming around the base of the trash can. A half-empty bottle of scotch sat on the floor next to the couch where I had a business engagement the night before.

She wanted to be a secretary. She had all the requirements — a great body that would make your back arch, and she made

a great cup of coffee. I gave her a job. That was yesterday.

San Francisco is a beautiful city . . . the cable cars, fog rolling off the bay, China-town, the Golden Gate Bridge, the wharf. Gee, I wish I lived there.

Being a private dick isn't easy with a name like Sam Spayed. It takes a special breed to be in my line of work. The hours are long, the pay stinks, and you can't trust anyone. It's not a pretty job. But, I've got all the requirements. I like babes and bullets . . . and, I look good in a trench coat.

"More coffee, Sam?"

It was a slow day. The hours seemed to drag by like a Cubs vs. Braves double-header. I decided to get a phone. As I was leaving the office, I found myself face-to-face with one of the most beautiful creatures I'd ever seen. Her ears were like the pyramids of Egypt; her eyes were limpid pools of gray with coal black slits; her whiskers swayed in the brisk, city breeze like cattails on a frog pond in southern Louisiana in September . . . sometime toward evening before ten and probably after eight-thirty . . . uh, where was I? Oh, yeah, the broad. She was cute.

"Are you Spayed?"

I never know how to answer that question.

So, why had she come to see me? What mysterious problem drove her to a Private Investigator? And, why me? There were a hundred Private Investigators in town with better offices than mine. Who was she? I decided to find out . . .

"So, what brings you here? And, why me? There are a hundred P.I.'s in town with better offices than mine. Who are you?

"My husband was murdered. You're cheap. Tanya O'Tabby. Will you take the case?"

I had to think for a min — "SURE!"

"How do you want your services paid, Mr. Spayed?"

"That would be great!"

My mind took off like a greyhound after a rabbit at Raceway Park. She *was* attractive and *young*. Judging from the way she was dressed, she was obviously tapping some big bucks. How would a girl get her hands on money like that? Of course! It all makes sense, now. She marries an old geezer, has him killed, and inherits all the money. She hires a second-rate investigator to find the killer, who she doublecrosses, and ends up scot free.

"So, how old was your husband, Mrs. O'Tabby?"

"Twenty-three."

Of course! It all makes sense, now. Her husband was obviously a ladies' man. He probably had felines in every alley. An Irish cat is known for his promiscuous nature. Tanya finds out he's unfaithful and has him snuffed. She hires a second-rate detective to find the killer, who she doublecrosses, and ends up scot free. It's one of the oldest shams in the book.

"So, what did your husband do for a living, Mrs. O'Tabby?"

"He was a priest."

Something wasn't right here.

"Wait a minute, doll. I thought priests weren't allowed to get married."

"He was Greek Orthodox, Mr. Spayed."

Of course, a Greek Orthodox priest named O'Tabby. It all made sense now.

"Call me Sam, please. What makes you think your husband was murdered?"

"He drove off Old Mountain Road, Sam Please. That's 40 miles away. He had no reason to be there. Besides, he was an excellent driver."

Her lips started to tremble. I took her paws in mine.

"Go home, kid. I've got work to do. I'll call you when I've got something."

Why someone would murder a twenty-three-year-old priest was beyond me. Still, stranger things have happened in this town.

My first stop was the city morgue. It would be a few days before the funeral, so his body should still be in the condition it was when he was found. The entire story Tanya had told me sounded like nothing more than an unfortunate accident. But, her sincerity was no act. She believed that her husband was murdered. She didn't know how or why, but then, that's my job.

It was 11:00 A.M.

Walking up the steps to the morgue, I saw my old adversary. It was Lieutenant Theotis Washington. Everytime he crossed my path, it was bad luck. He was a black cat.

"Spayed! What brings you down here? Trying to find a client?"

"Sure Lieutenant. He's the one your blue boys shot in the back for J-walking."

"Watch it Spayed. I still have your license under investigation."

"Oh, yeah. Well, at least I know it's safe for awhile."

"Spayed, don't push me!"

"Wouldn't dream of it Lieutenant. Have a nice day!"

The Lieutenant was still saying good-byes as I walked into the morgue. I spotted an old friend, Burt Fleebish. He'd been working there ever since I was a snotty-nosed kitten.

"Sam, what brings you down here?"

"Hey, Burt, I need to see a body."

"Who doesn't, eh, Sam? What's the name?

"Father O'Tabby"

"Oh, yeah! Tough break . . . nice fella . . ."

"You knew him?"

"Oh, not really. I attended his church, St. Morris, for about the last six months. We'd talk occasionally after services."

I could tell Burt sort of liked the guy by the way he pulled out the drawer with the stiff.

Tabby looked like he'd been worked over by the Maulers of the Midway. It didn't surprise me. What was a guy supposed to look like when he goes through a guardrail fence, and down a mountain canyon in his car. If his body hadn't been thrown out of the car while it was rolling over, it would have been burned up when the car caught fire and exploded.

"When's the autopsy scheduled, Burt?"

"Autopsy, what autopsy?"

"His wife thinks it was murder, Burt."

"Murder! Sam, the man died in a disastrous car accident. It's as simple as that!"

"Burt, if things were as simple as that, I wouldn't have a job."

Looking down at O'Tabby, I noticed some yellowish-brown coloration on his chest and stomach hairs.

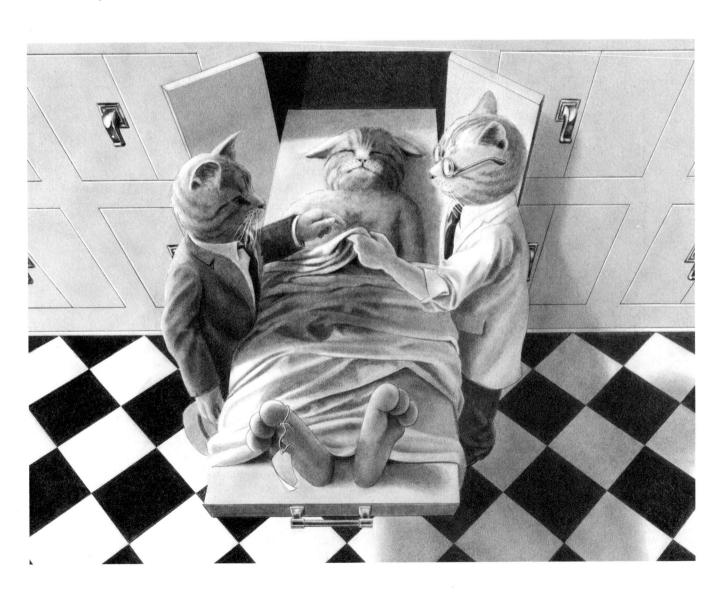

"Hey, Burt. Do you have any explanation for this?" I pointed out the pigment in question.

"Oh, could be almost anything — transmission fluid, brake fluid. Any kind of liquid from a car can make a stain like that."

"Do you have his clothes and any items he had on him when he was discovered?"

"Oh, sure, Sam. Right here."

He handed me a plastic bag filled mostly with his torn, shredded and blood-stained clothes. I searched through the clothing looking for anything that might suggest murder. Right now, it looked as though poor O'Tabby just had a bad break on the mountain.

His shirt was about the only item of clothing that was still recognizable; although, it was badly ripped and blood-stained. I noticed the yellowish-brown stains were in the same location on the shirt that they were on the body. I had seen stains like this before. But, where? Maybe something would come to me later.

The pockets were empty, except for the stones and dirt from the fall down the mountain. There was a curious little stone in the vest pocket. It was very colorful on one side, almost as though it were painted.

The phone rang. As Burt went to answer it, I put the colorful stone in my pocket. I don't know why really. Maybe I just liked stones.

Burt hung up the phone and asked if there was anything else I needed before he put the body away.

"A clue, a motive, and a murderer. Goodnight Burt."

"Sam..."

"Yeah, Burt?"

"It's noon."

Next on the list was Father O'Tabby's church. I was still a couple of blocks from the church when I brushed by a big goon on the sidewalk with fists the size of babies. He grabbed me by the throat, drug me into a darkened alley and pounded me into next year. As I lay there in a crumpled heap, I smiled to myself. I must be on the trail of something hot to rate a beating from this Neanderthal. I put my jaw back in place and pointed an accusing paw at my assailant.

"So, Clyde ... I suppose you have a message for me."

"Yeah, I'm your landlord. You're two months late with the rent."

"Right."

I was still trying to figure out my landlord's involvement in this caper, as I walked up the marble steps to the church. At the doorway, I was greeted by an elderly man wearing a robe.

"Are you the Father here?"

"Yes, but I have no children."

"What?"

"I'm sorry. That's a small, religious joke. Yes, I'm Father O'Felix. How may I help you?"

"I'm Sam Spayed, P.I." I held up my wallet.

"Nice wallet, Mr. P.I."

"I'd like to ask you a few questions about Father O'Tabby."

"Certainly, Mr. P.I. Why don't you come inside."

I entered the church and followed O'Felix to the kitchen. I sat at the table as the Father poured us a cup of coffee. I would have preferred to have my own cup.

"What would you like to know, Mr. P.I.?"

"Call me Sam. Was O'Tabby a good driver?"

"Oh, yes. He was a drivers training instructor at Edison High in the summer months."

"Do you have any idea why O'Tabby was on the Old Mountain Road last Friday night?"

"Yes, he was going to visit Maudie O'Purr, one of our parishioners. She is a wealthy hermit who has been ailing of late."

"Why was he going there?"

"Maudie is a big contributor to the church. Father O'Tabby called on her every

Friday night to help in any way he could."

"Does anyone else know this?"

"It was Maudie's wish that no one know of his visits."

Did he have any enemies you knew of, Father?"

"What are you getting at, Sam?"

"Just the facts, Father."

"Father O'Tabby was loved by everyone who knew him, especially the female parishoners."

"What do you mean by that?"

"Just that he was an attractive man, and it was natural for women to be attracted to him."

Of course!

"How old is Maudie O'Purr?"

"Ninety-three."

"Rats."

Father O'Felix shifted restlessly in his chair.

"Sam, I meant nothing carnal by my statement. However, on more than one occasion Father O'Tabby had to put a woman's feelings in perspective."

"So, you don't think he ever gave in to temptation?"

"Oh, no. His only weakness was coffee. I rarely saw him without a cup of it in his hand."

"Yeah. Well, I think we all depend on a cup of Joe every now and then.

"Thank's for the information. And, no offense intended, but *this* is really lousy coffee."

"Yes, I admit my coffee needs work. Sam. The lady that normally makes our coffee left us recently. She made excellent coffee. She's going to be hard to replace. In fact, I find myself doing her duties more often than my own."

"I see. Well, nice meeting you."

It was only a few blocks back to my office. By the time I arrived, the men from the phone company had just installed my phone and were on their way out. Kitty was in the other room.

"No calls yet, Sam. How about a cup of coffee?"

I sat down at my desk and stared at the phone. I thought I'd better call Tanya and let her know the progress on the case. Maybe she could give me something else to go on.

"Hey, Kitty. Do we have Tanya's phone number?"

"555-1234, Sam."

"Thanks."

The girl might not be a great office cleaner, but she has a great memory. But, why didn't I remember that number? It's sure an easy one to remember.

"Hello. Tanya . . . Sam Spayed."

"Mr. Spayed, what did you find out?"

"Not much, really. Look, I stopped by your husband's church today and found out a few interesting things."

"Oh really, who did you talk with?"

"A Father O'Felix . . . do you know him?"

"Of course, Father O'Felix was my husband's assistant."

"Kind of old to be an assistant, isn't he?"

"Oh, we really never thought of him as an assistant. He worked as hard as my husband with the congregation. In fact, he's been with the church all his life."

Kitty was setting the cup of coffee down on my desk.

"Well, anyway, Tanya. He mentioned your husband may have had some woman trouble at the church and . . ."

CRASH!

"Damn it. That's hot!"

Kitty had dropped the cup of coffee on my desk and into my lap. It was hot enough to give a literal meaning to my last name. The cup had broken into several pieces on the desk.

"Sam, hello, Sam are you okay?"

"Look Tanya, I'll call you back. We've got a bit of a mess right now."

I hung up.

"Sam, I'm so sorry! I don't know what I was thinking about."

"It's okay, Kitty. Run downstairs and tell maintenance we need a mop and bucket. I'll pick up the pieces of the mug."

I could tell she was really upset about the mess. Hell, it was only coffee. Anyone can make a mistake. No problem. I'd fire her when she came back.

I was soaked. I went to the sink to clean up. As I took off my vest, I saw a huge coffee stain covering my shirt. Wait a minute! Coffee stains! That's what they were. O'Tabby had coffee stains on his shirt! Why would a man that was dressed as impecabbly as O'Tabby wear a coffee-stained shirt? Where did the coffee come from? *And,* why am I talking to myself? I searched my vest pockets for the pretty, painted stone I took from O'Tabby's vest pocket. I looked at it carefully. It was painted, alright . . . a painted, piece of ceramic! A piece of ceramic from a coffee cup! O'Tabby must have been drinking coffee, which in turn caused the accident. It wasn't much to go on. How was I supposed to solve a murder when my only clue was a cup of java?

What was keeping Kitty? Funny, she didn't seem to be the awkward type. I figured I'd better call Tanya to apologize for the interruption and to get back to the case.

Where did I put the phone number? Wait a minute. Tanya never gave me a phone number. So, how did Kitty know the number? Easy, Spayed, don't go off the deep end. But, the pieces were starting to fit together. Kitty would know the number if Tanya's *husband* gave it to her. Could she be one of the felines infatuated with Father O'Tabby that Father O'Felix mentioned? Think Spayed, think. Of course! She spilled the coffee when I mentioned talking to Father O'Felix about O'Tabby's woman trouble. Kitty makes a great cup of coffee. So did the girl who recently left the church. The same girl I hired only yesterday. A girl who was infatuated by a man she could never have.

So, what does she do? She spills coffee in his lap and drives him over a cliff . . . something is not quite right here.

"Here's maintenance, Sam."

It was Kitty with an old tom cat carry-ing a pail and mop.

"I know you murdered Father O'Tab-by, Kitty."

"What are you talking about, Sam?"

"You loved him, he didn't love you, you couldn't have him. So . . . you snuffed him."

She fell to her knees sobbing. "Yes, I loved him. He didn't love me, I couldn't have him, so I . . ."

"So you, what?"

"So I left."

"You left?"

"Yes, the thought of working at the church, so close to him and not being able to have him was too much to bear. So, I left. But, I didn't murder him."

The tears were streaming down her face and falling off her whiskers like rain off a pine tree.

"But, the coffee stains . . . the painted piece of ceramic coffee cup?" I held the

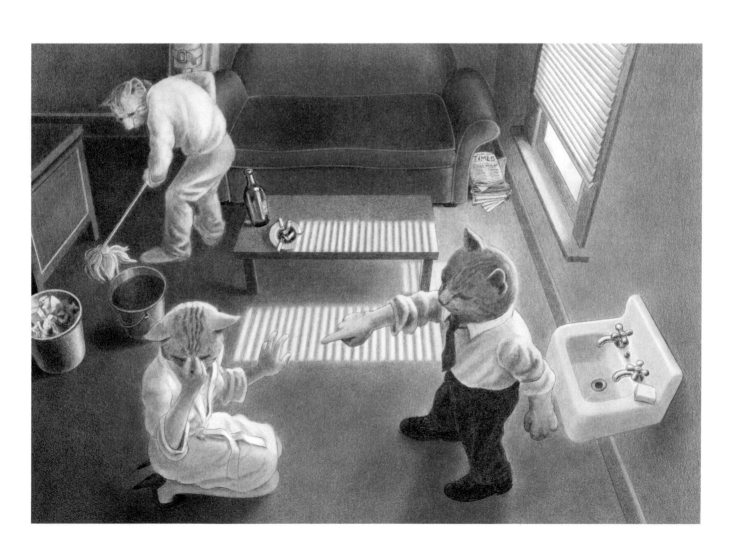

ceramic piece out to her quivering paws.

"We talked a few nights before his death at the church. We had some coffee." The crying stopped. "He liked my coffee."

I had to agree with O'Tabby. Kitty made a great cup of coffee.

"He always drank from his favorite mug, Sam." She took the ceramic piece from my paw. "This looks like a piece from that mug. I don't know how it got broke."

I just ran out of suspects.

"Kitty, did you have any duties at the church other than making coffee?"

"I was Father O'Tabby's Girl Friday."

"You certainly weren't his Girl Saturday."

"Put a cork in it, Sam."

"Sorry."

"I sorted out his mail, answered the phone, filled his prescriptions, cleaned his robes . . ."

"Wait a minute! Filled his prescriptions?!"

"Yes, Father O'Tabby was an insom-

niac. The coffee kept him awake. He needed very potent sleeping pills to help him doze off at night."

Her expression softened to a sweet smile as she gazed into the distance.

"I remember him bragging that one of those pills could knock out a bull elephant. It took two to put him to sleep, and that took an hour."

"Kitty, stay here and help maintenance clean up this mess."

"Where are you going, Sam?"

"To pick up a murderer, baby."

I was packing my piece, although I didn't think I'd need it this time. It was pouring rain when I got outside. No matter, I was only going a few blocks.

The marble steps looked cold and gray—almost depressing. Not what you'd expect at the front of a church. It was 4:00 P.M.

When I found Father O'Felix, he was kneeling before the altar. His head was bowed and his paws clasped in prayer.

"Asking for forgiveness, Father?"

His head turned slowly. Wet streaks from his eyes to his mouth were on his furry face. It looked as though he had been crying for some time.

"I'm not worthy of being a Father," he continued sobbing.

"And, you don't have the equipment to be a mother."

"What?"

"Sorry, pal, that's a small, religious joke. Let's go."

By the time the paperwork was done, it was 8:00 P.M. Lt. Washington was his usual charmer, as O'Felix was being booked. It had been a long day. I thought I'd better check on Kitty. She was pretty shaken up when I left. As I walked back to the office, I noticed the rain had stopped . . . it was snowing. I entered my office and found Tanya O'Tabby sitting on the couch. She stood up slowly, sobbing, gently put her arms around me. She didn't say anything. She didn't have to. I understood. She stopped hugging me and smiled softly. She

gave me an envelope and walked quietly out of my life.

"She called after you'd left." It was Kitty in the kitchen. "I told her you were going to nab the murderer. She came right over."

I didn't answer. My thoughts were still in the arms of a classy puss. There had better be a check in that envelope.

"Sam, how did you know Father O'Felix killed Father O'Tabby?"

"O'Tabby had to have left directly from the church to call on Maudie O'Purr that night, because he was still drinking from his favorite mug when the crash occurred. Father O'Felix, the substitute girl Friday, fixed that cup of coffee. O'Felix had filled O'Tabby's sleeping pill prescription and popped a couple into his coffee knowing it would take O'Tabby an hour to get to Old Mountain Road 40 miles away. Like clockwork, O'Tabby fell asleep at the wheel and drove off the road." The motive was obvious."

"Which was?"

"It was the old, power struggle in the church routine, Kitty. Old man gets passed over by younger man. Young man gets power, notoriety, women, money. Old man gets older, bitter. Finally, out of frustration, the old man gets rid of only thing in his way . . . the young man. With O'Tabby gone, O'Felix becomes pastor and gets what has eluded him all his life."

Kitty came out of the kitchen holding a bottle of my favorite scotch and two glasses.

"Sam, you're simply too much." She closed the door to the office.

"What's the scotch for, Kitty?"

She set the bottle on the floor next to the couch and turned out the light.

THE EXTERMINATORS

Written by: Jim Davis

Illustrated by: Jim Davis, Mike Fentz, and Larry Fentz

THE
EXTERMINATORS

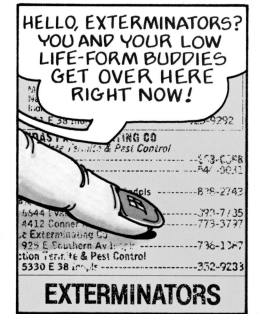

LAB ANIMAL

Written by: Jim Davis
Illustrated by: Gary Barker and Larry Fentz

LAB ANIMAL

243517

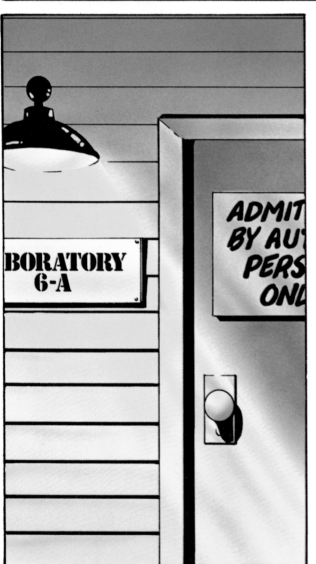

BORATORY
6-A

ADMIT
BY AU
PERS
ONL

RAPID
BIOGENETIC
MUTATION

UNITED STATES
GOVERNMENT
RESEARCH
FACILITY
★ RESTRICTED ★

19-GB

LARRY, GET 19-GB READY FOR DISSECTION. WE'LL SEE IF IT'S EXPERIENCED ANY PRELIMINARY ORGAN MODIFICATION

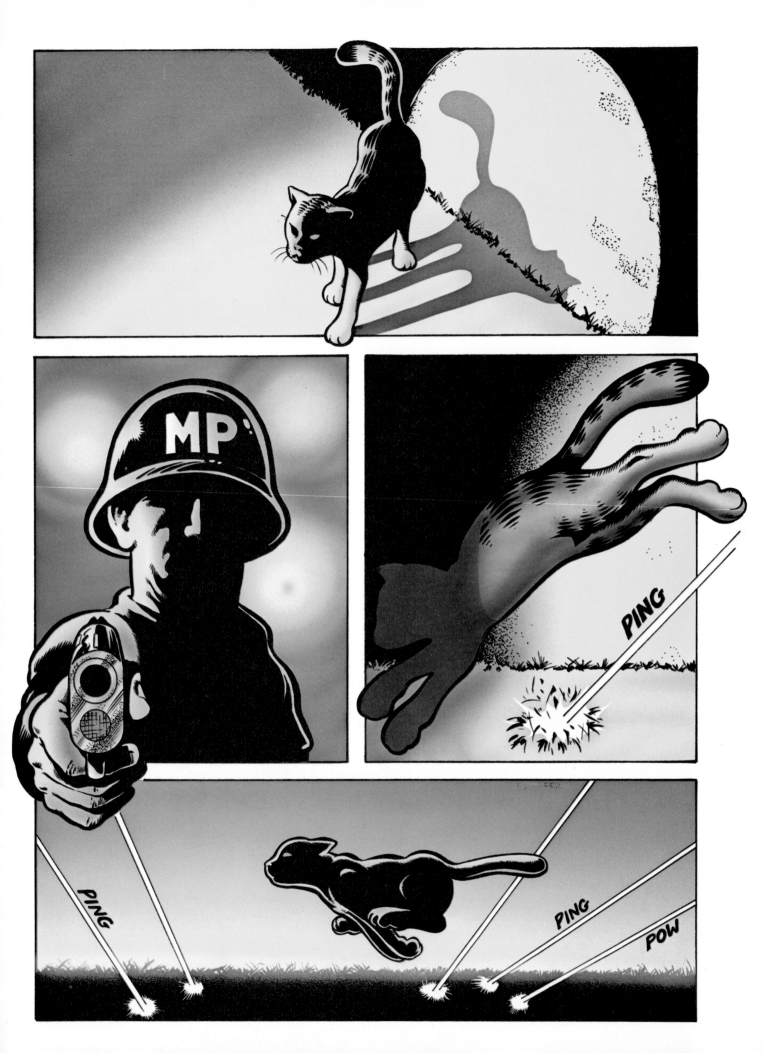

"LET'S CALL IT OFF. WE'LL NEVER FIND HIM NOW"

THE GARDEN
Written and Illustrated by: Dave Kühn

The Garden

Yellow and orange skies
filled with magic butterflies
made the morning a memory.
These were the mornings Cloey
and the orange kitten liked best.

It seemed like it was always summer in the garden. Uncle Tod built the garden during a very intense period of just having fun. He was known for that.

Singing and dancing and being every bit a prankster, he and the sun laughed alot.

Uncle Tod joined the circus one spring and sort of willed the garden to Cloey and the orange kitten.
From then on, the spirit of Uncle Tod seemed to loom over the plot like a laughing apparition.

This was not the normal garden
you might imagine... no,
it was inspired by the love of life
and the even greater love of living it.
The garden had a few of the more
identifiable features, plants,
rocks, and some fencing. But, the
things that they really
enjoyed were not
of the norm.

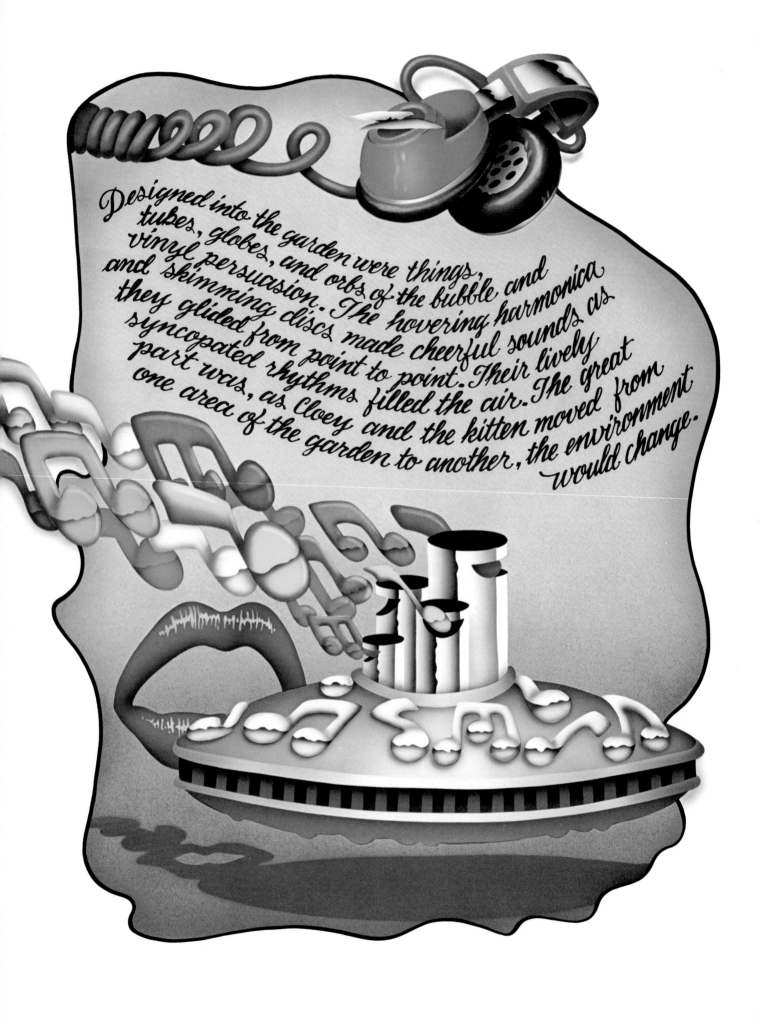

Designed into the garden were things, tubes, globes, and orbs of the bubble and vinyl persuasion. The hovering harmonica and skimming discs made cheerful sounds as they glided from point to point. Their lively syncopated rhythms filled the air. The great part was, as Cloey and the kitten moved from one area of the garden to another, the environment would change.

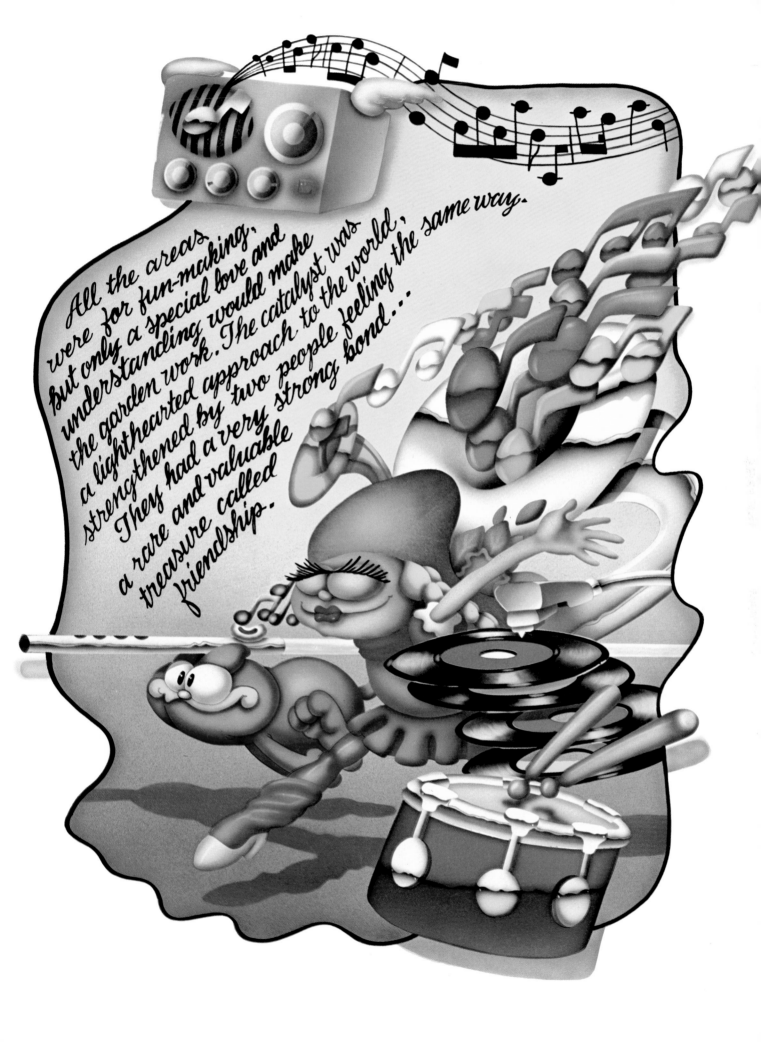

All the areas,
were for fun-making,
but only a special love and
understanding would make
the garden work. The catalyst was
a lighthearted approach to the world,
strengthened by two people feeling the same way.
They had a very strong bond...
a rare and valuable
treasure called
friendship.

So, Cloey and the kitten would wisk themselves away ever so easily into Uncle Tod's garden of delights as long as they retained their beautiful way of feeling.

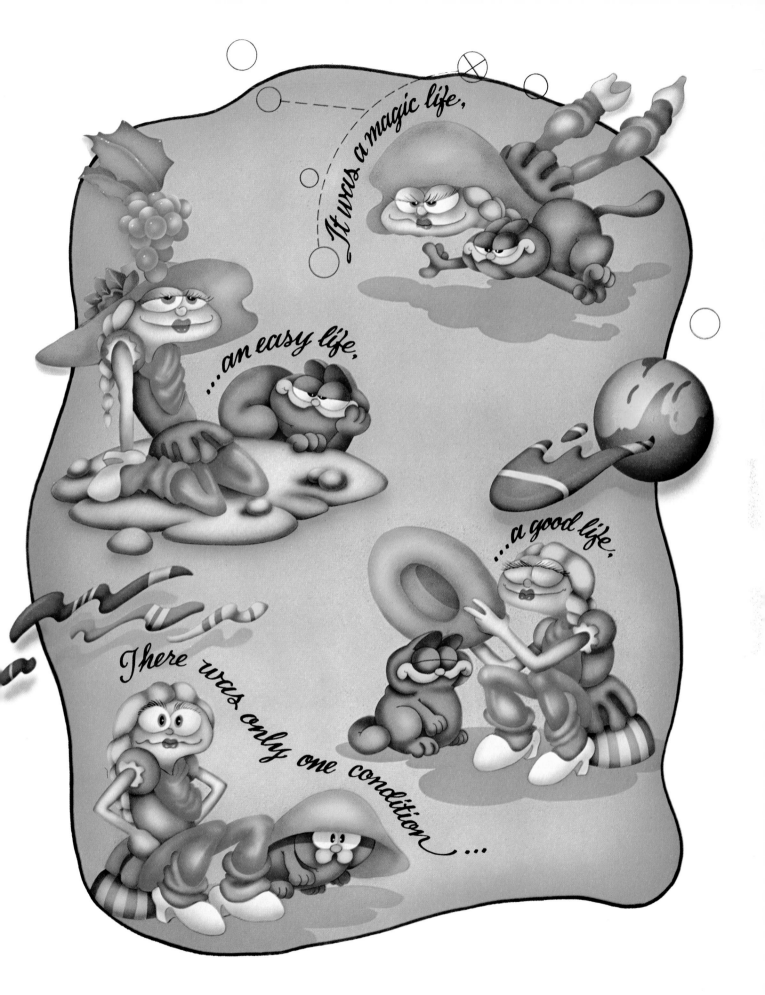

As all children want to do, Cloey and the kitten were overcome with curiosity. They poked at the crystal box, sniffed it, and gazed longingly at the simple-to-open latch. There is something very special about a box that is not to be opened. Finally they decided to take action!

They decided NOT to open it! They danced right by the crystal box, never to give it another moment's thought. They loved Uncle Tod very, very much and were grateful for the garden he provided for them. They would never do anything to hurt him.

And they lived happily forever, and ever, and ever, and ever, and ever...

PRIMAL SELF
Written by: Jim Davis
Illustrated by: Jim Clements, Gary Barker, and Larry Fentz

TIGGER

TIGGER

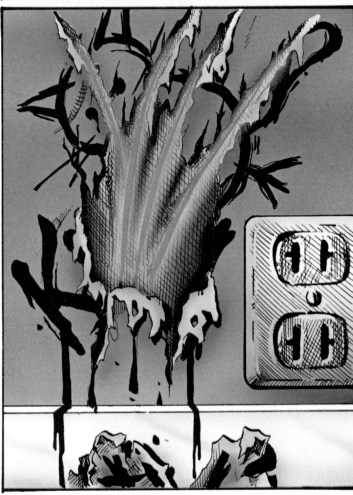

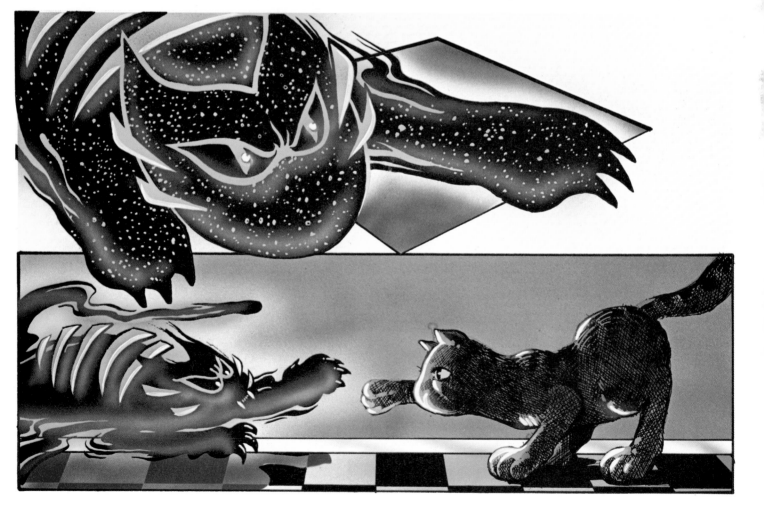

GARFIELD

Written by: Jim Davis
Illustrated by: Gary Barker and Valette Hildebrand
Color: Doc Davis

JUNE 19, 1978

MEROOOOOOOOO

WELCOME TO THE WORLD, LITTLE FELLOW. I THINK I'LL CALL YOU GARFIELD

I'M HUNGRY!

WHERE ARE WE, MOM?

IN THE KITCHEN OF AN ITALIAN RESTAURANT

ARE ITALIANS GOOD TO EAT? OOF!

YOU HAVE A LOT TO LEARN, GARFIELD

GARFIELD, THE NEWBORN KITTEN, IS GETTING READY TO RUB UP AGAINST HIS FIRST LEG. ON MY MARK, GET SET...

RUB UP!

ARRRRGH!

THIS IS FUN!

WHUMP

ARRRRGH! WHAT'S THAT?!

THAT'S A DOG. PEOPLE ACTUALLY BUY THEM AND TAKE THEM HOME FOR PETS

HELLO THERE. I'D LIKE TO BUY A CAT

TAKE ME! TAKE ME! I'LL CATCH YOUR MICE, FETCH YOUR PAPER, SCRATCH YOUR BACK. I'LL BE SWEET, LICK YOUR FEET AND FIX A SNACK. TAKE ME!

SHOOP

THIS ONE SEEMS FRIENDLY

I SLEEP TIL NOON AND DESIRE MY MILK TEPID. I REQUIRE THREE DAILY SCRATCHINGS AND I EAT A PASTA BASED DIET. NO SUBSTITUTIONS, PLEASE. AS FAR AS ACCOMODATIONS, MY BED MUST BE...

HOW ARE YOU THIS MORNING, GARFIELD?

I'M IN A GOOD MOOD. I LET THE MAILMAN LIVE

SIT DOWN, GARFIELD. I HAVE SOMETHING TO TELL YOU

I **AM** SITTING DOWN

YOU MUST BE LONELY. I THINK YOU NEED A PLAYMATE

NOT REALLY, I HAVE MY MIRROR

SO I BOUGHT A DOG

ARRRGH!

SPACE CAT
Written and Illustrated by: Jim Clements

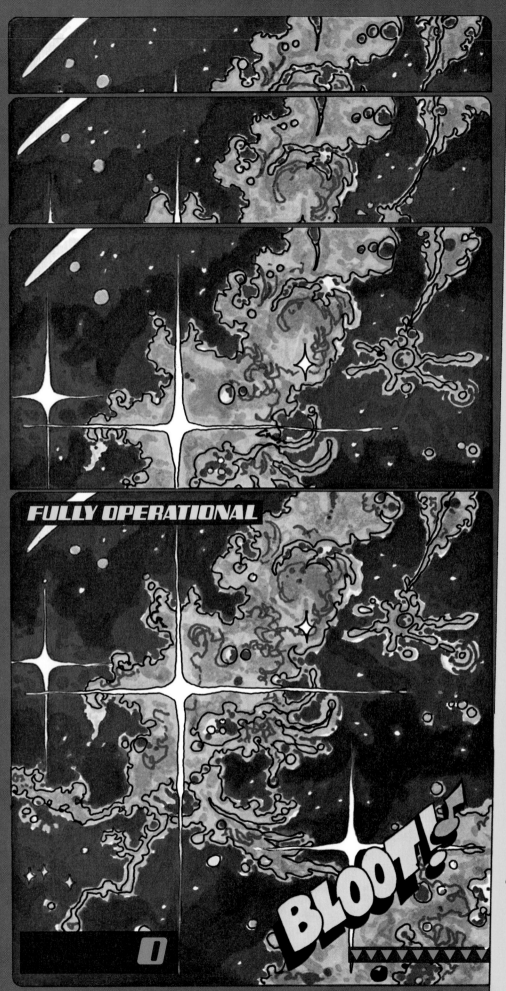

SPACE...

ONE THING TO BE SAID FOR SPACE, THERE SURE IS A LOT OF IT OUT THERE.

SPACE ISN'T LIKE YOU OR ME. SPACE PLAYS BY ITS OWN RULES AND YOU EITHER GO ALONG WITH THOSE RULES OR SPACE GETS TICKED. AND WHEN SPACE GETS TICKED IT PICKS UP ITS BALL AND GOES HOME! SO WHAT DO YOU DO WITH SPACE? WELL, IN THE TECHNOLOGICAL GREATNESS OF THE FUTURE YOU DO HAVE CHOICES. YOU CAN TAKE PART IN GRAND INTERGALACTIC BATTLES THAT ENCOMPASS WHOLE SOLAR SYSTEMS. OR YOU CAN BRAVELY FORGE NEW WORLDS OF EXPLORATION BY TRAVELING THROUGH UNCHARTED TERRITORY.

OR YOU CAN GET LOST.

ME?

I'M LOST.

I'M NOT JUST ANY LOST EITHER. I'M ONE OF THOSE GOOD SOLID "GOD I'M DOOMED" TYPE OF LOSTS. THIS IS A LOST YOU CAN BE PROUD OF!

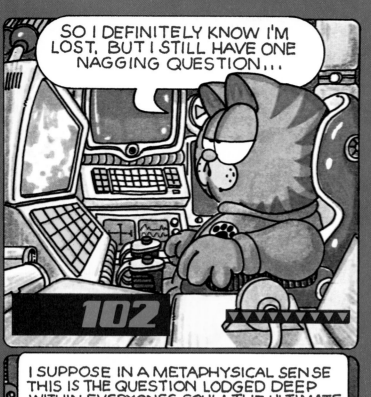

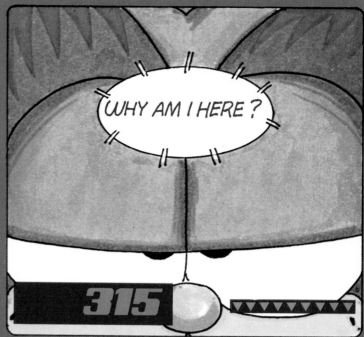

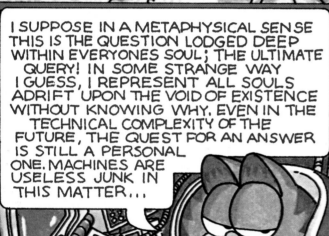

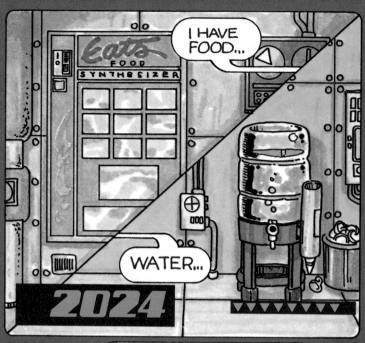

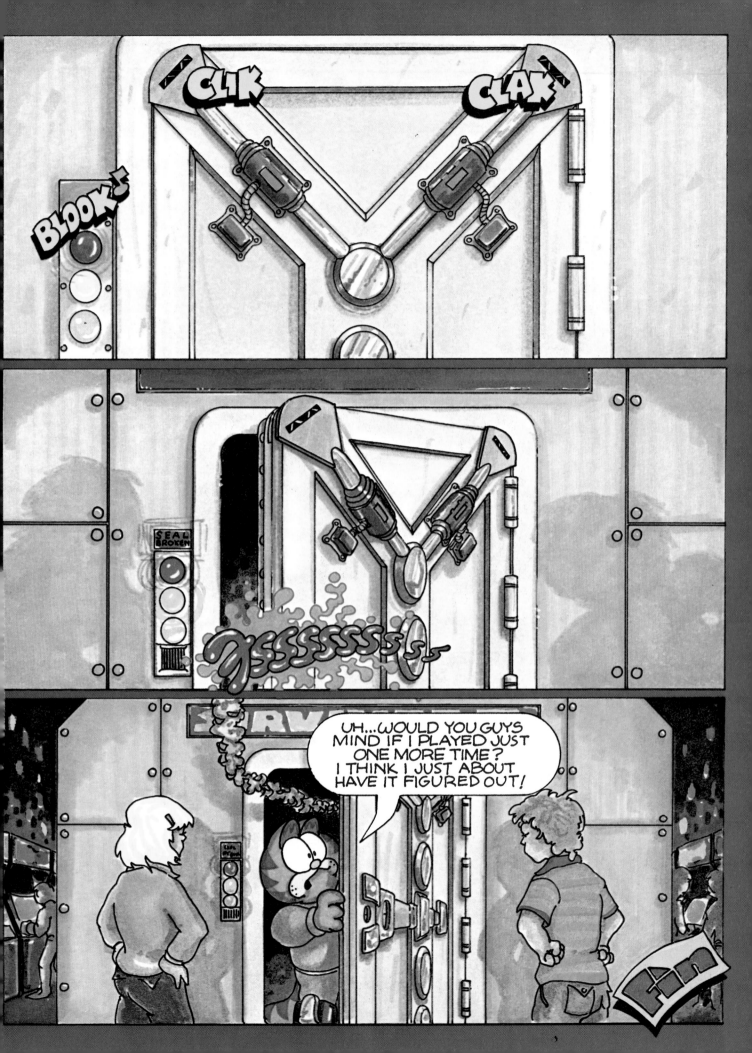